BUILDING BLOCKS OF PHYSICAL SCIENCE

ELECTRICITY

Written by Joseph Midthun

Illustrated by Samuel Hiti

a Scott Fetzer company
Chicago

World Book, Inc.
180 North LaSalle Street
Suite 900
Chicago, Illinois 60601
USA

For information about other World Book publications, visit our website at **www.worldbook.com** or call **1-800-WORLDBK (967-5325).**
For information about sales to schools and libraries, call 1-800-975-3250 (United States), or 1-800-837-5365 (Canada).

Library of Congress Cataloging-in-Publication Data for this volume has been applied for.

Building Blocks of Physical Science
ISBN: 978-0-7166-4460-6 (set, hc.)

Electricity
ISBN: 978-0-7166-4461-3 (hc.)

Also available as:
ISBN: 978-0-7166-4471-2 (e-book)

1st printing March 2022

Acknowledgments:
Created by Samuel Hiti and Joseph Midthun
Art by Samuel Hiti
Additional art by David Shephard/ The Bright Agency
Additional spot art by Dreamstime and Shutterstock
Text by Joseph Midthun

TABLE OF CONTENTS

There is a glossary on page 39. Terms defined in the glossary are in type **that looks like this** on their first appearance.

WHAT IS ELECTRICITY?

HEY!

I'm Electricity!

I'm a form of energy.

Energy makes things move and do work!

People use me to do all kinds of work...

I power lights...
8:00

Electronics...
8:01

And many kinds of machines.

I even power you!

But you have to be careful around me. If you get too close, you might get shocked!

ELECTRICITY IN NATURE

Electricity is a part of nature.

Sometimes, you can see me on a stormy night.

Lightning is pure electricity!

Actually, electricity is a part of *all* **matter.**

CRACKA-BOOM

I'm inside you right now.

Every action and every thought are a result of electricity.

Electrical signals inside your body carry information to and from your brain.

These signals tell your brain what your eyes see, what your ears hear...

...and what your fingers feel.

The signals even tell your heart when to beat!
PUM PUM
PUM PUM

ALL CHARGED UP
All matter is made of tiny particles called **atoms.**
ATOM

Atoms are made of even tinier particles.
Particles that carry a positive charge or neutral charge make up the center of an atom.

Electrons are negatively charged particles that circle around the center of an atom.

When atoms have an equal number of positive and negative particles, they have no **electric charge.**
BOO-HOO!

But atoms can gain or lose electrons.

When this happens, an atom becomes electrically charged!

The movement of electrons is what we call electricity.

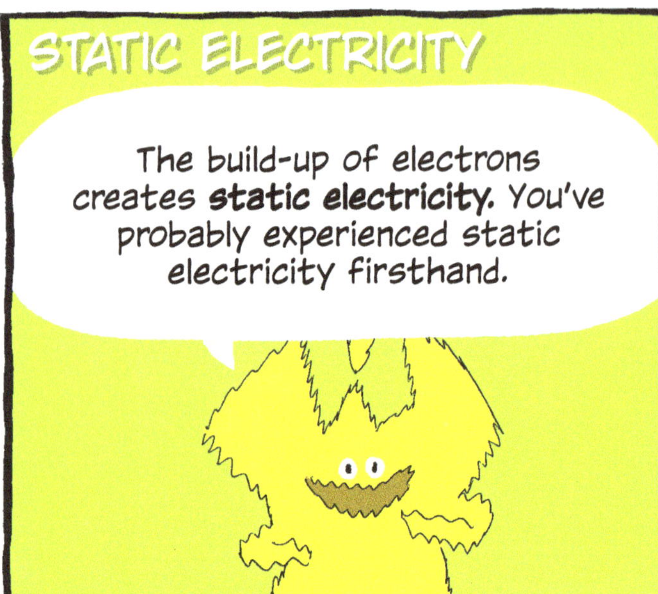
STATIC ELECTRICITY
The build-up of electrons creates **static electricity.** You've probably experienced static electricity firsthand.

Have you ever shuffled your feet across a carpet and then touched a doorknob?
Rub
Rub
Rub

What happened?
You probably got an electric shock!
ZAP

The rubbing between your feet and the rug causes electrons to jump from the rug to your body.

This gives your body extra electrons.
You get a negative charge!

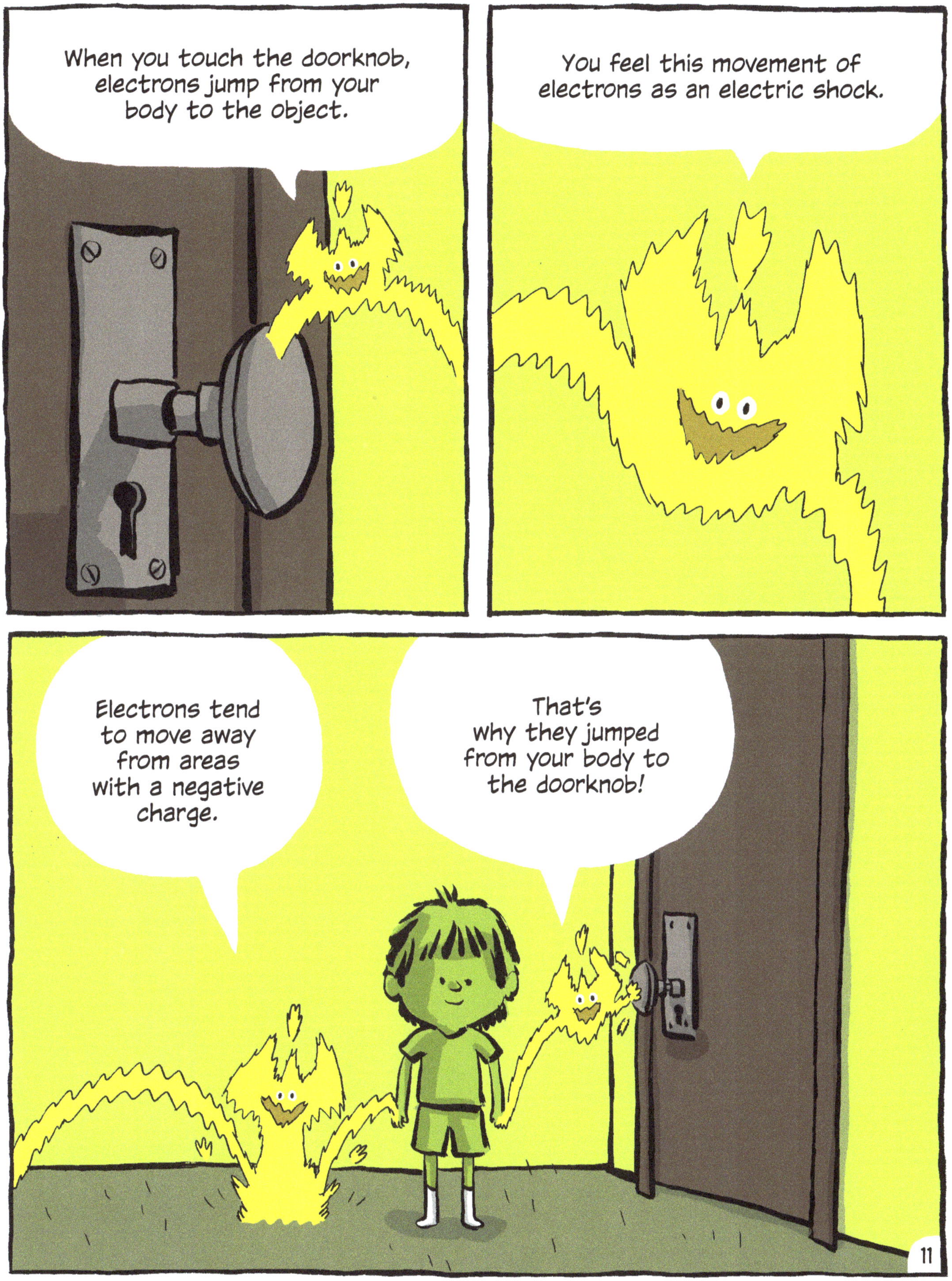

Electrons tend to move away from areas with a negative charge.

That's why they jumped from your body to the doorknob!

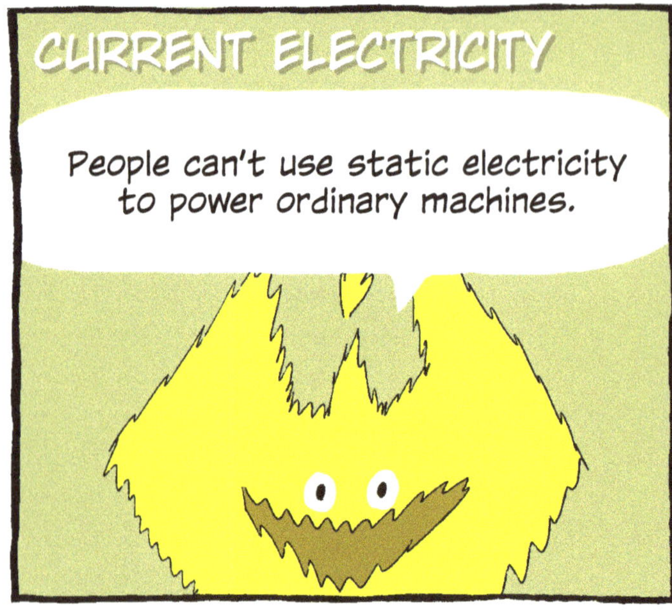
CURRENT ELECTRICITY
People can't use static electricity to power ordinary machines.

That's because the electric charge is released all at once.
POOM

To make electricity more useful, we must create an **electric current.**
ELECTRIC CURRENT

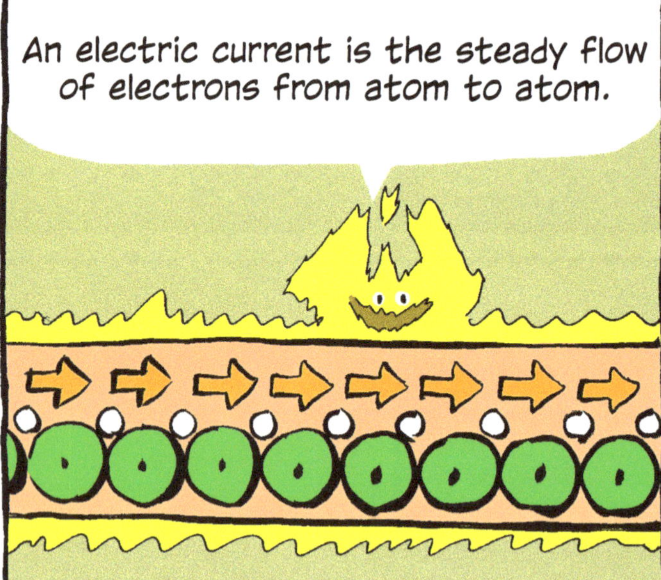
An electric current is the steady flow of electrons from atom to atom.

Electric current that we use for energy flows in a loop is called a **circuit.**

Think of a circuit as a raceway.
The cars are electrons that race around the track.
VROOM

Simple circuits have three main parts: an energy source, an object that needs electric current to work, and a wire that connects them.
circuit

This robot uses batteries as an energy source.

Energy is stored inside the battery's chemicals.
Battery

This energy pushes electrons through the circuit.
Battery

As the electrons flow, the robot moves!

CIRCUITS AND SWITCHES

Switches allow you to control the flow of current by opening and closing the circuit.

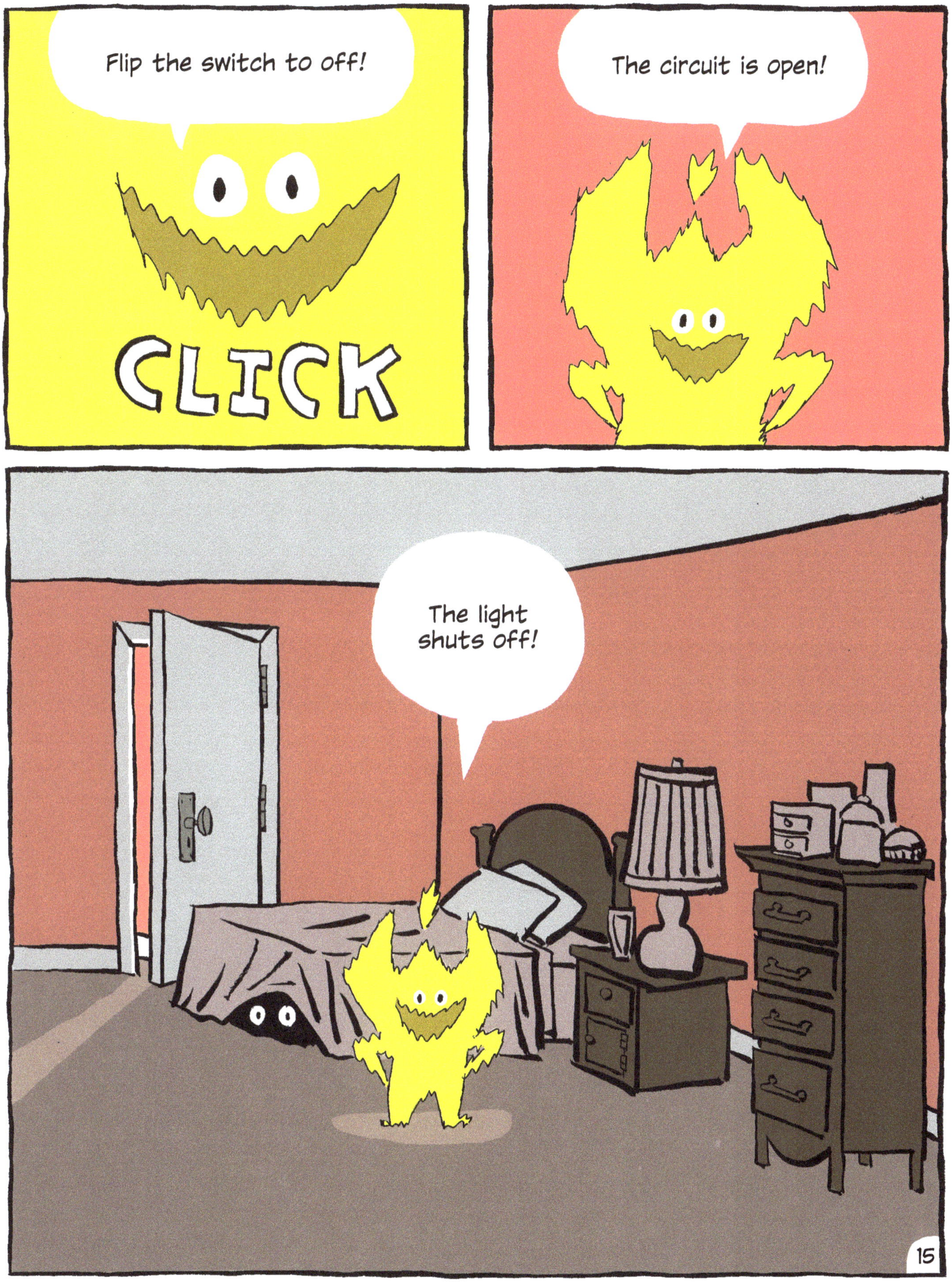

The light shuts off!

CONDUCTORS AND INSULATORS

Other materials stop the flow of electrons from atom to atom.
These materials are called **insulators.**
Wood, plastic, and rubber are good insulators.
Electrical wires are often covered by rubber or plastic.
These materials keep the electric current in the wire and prevent you from getting an electric shock!

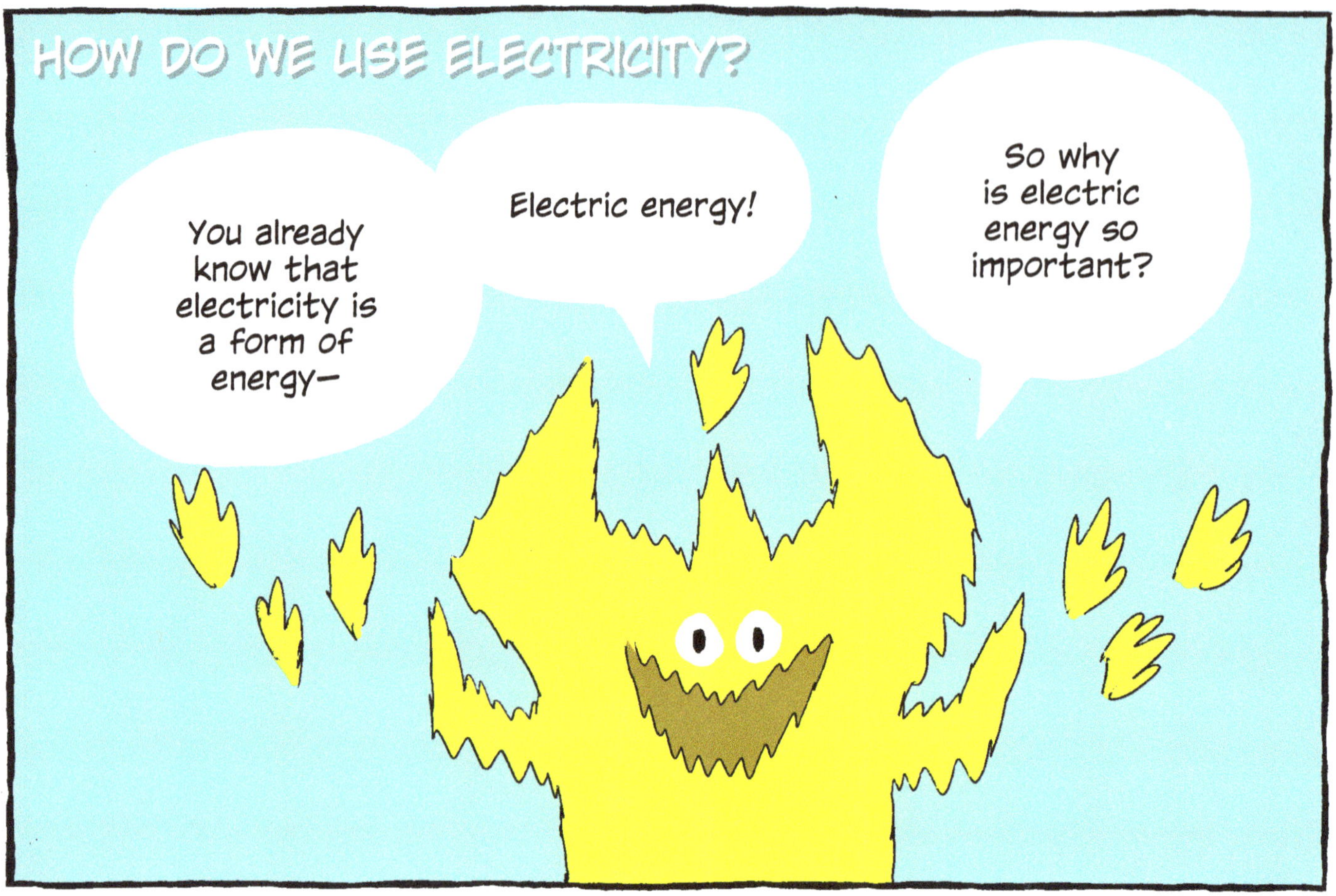

HOW DO WE USE ELECTRICITY?

You already know that electricity is a form of energy—

Electric energy!

So why is electric energy so important?

Because we can use it to make many other forms of energy.

Look at the lights around you.

They're using electric energy to make light energy!

The energy of **motion!**

These things are possible because of me!

GENERATING ELECTRICITY

People use a lot of electricity every day.

So where, you might ask, does all this electricity come from?

Power plants!

Power plants use **electric generators** to convert mechanical energy into electric energy.

These giant machines are driven by a **turbine.**

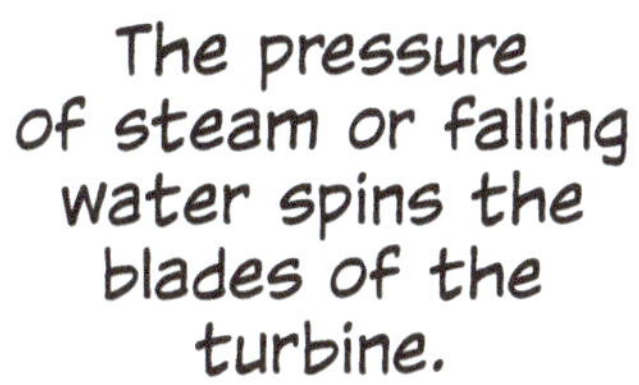

The pressure of steam or falling water spins the blades of the turbine.

The spinning blades cause magnets inside the generator to spin around a metal wire.

The spinning magnets push and pull on the electrons inside the wire.

The moving electrons create an electric current.

Power plants generate enough current to power entire cities!

Once an electric current is generated, it is directed into the electrical grid.
The electrical grid is a huge circuit.
It is made of power lines and connections that bring electricity to your home.
Your home is connected to the grid by copper wires wrapped in plastic.

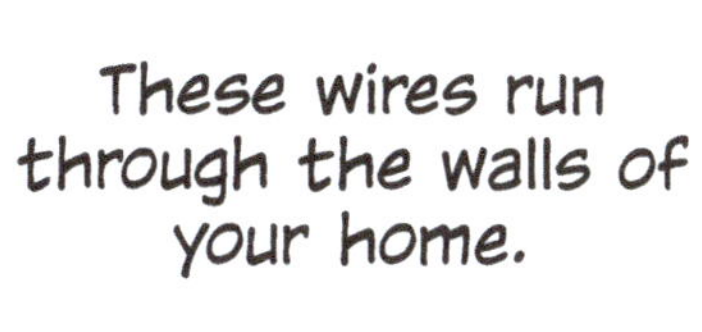
These wires run through the walls of your home.

People tap into the grid by plugging a cord into an outlet on the wall.

Presto! The circuit is complete!

THE INVENTION OF ELECTRIC POWER

A little over 100 years ago, people didn't have electricity in their homes.

In the 1800's, people learned to capture electricity and use it to do work.

Inventors and scientists discovered how to make large amounts of electric energy.

They found ways to use that energy to make light and heat.

This led to the invention of electric devices, or electronics.

Some devices allowed people to talk across great distances.
CLICK
HELLO?

Others helped people handle information quickly.
TIK
TIK
TIK

Over time, the demand for electricity grew.

Today, most people cannot imagine life without electric power.
But there are negative effects to all this energy use...

SOURCES OF ELECTRIC POWER

Most of the electric energy we use comes from power plants. Some plants burn **fossil fuels** to generate electric power. Others use **nuclear fuel.**

Fossil fuels were formed from the remains of living things that died millions of years ago. *Nuclear fuel* releases the plentiful energy created by splitting certain kinds of atoms.

Many people are worried about the dangerous waste that nuclear fuels leave. They also worry that the supply of fossil fuels will run out one day.

On top of that, burning these fossil fuels harms our planet.

Scientists have learned how to convert energy from other sources as well.

For instance, this dam uses the power of running water to generate electricity.

And when wind turns the blades of a windmill, a turbine creates electricity!

Solar panels convert the sun's energy directly into electricity.
Soak up those rays!

REDUCING ELECTRICITY USE

Today, there are more people on Earth than ever before.

And because there are more and more objects that need electricity to work...

...the demand for electric power continues to grow.

So it is important to reduce your electricity use.

Why not open the shades instead of turning on a light?

ZIP

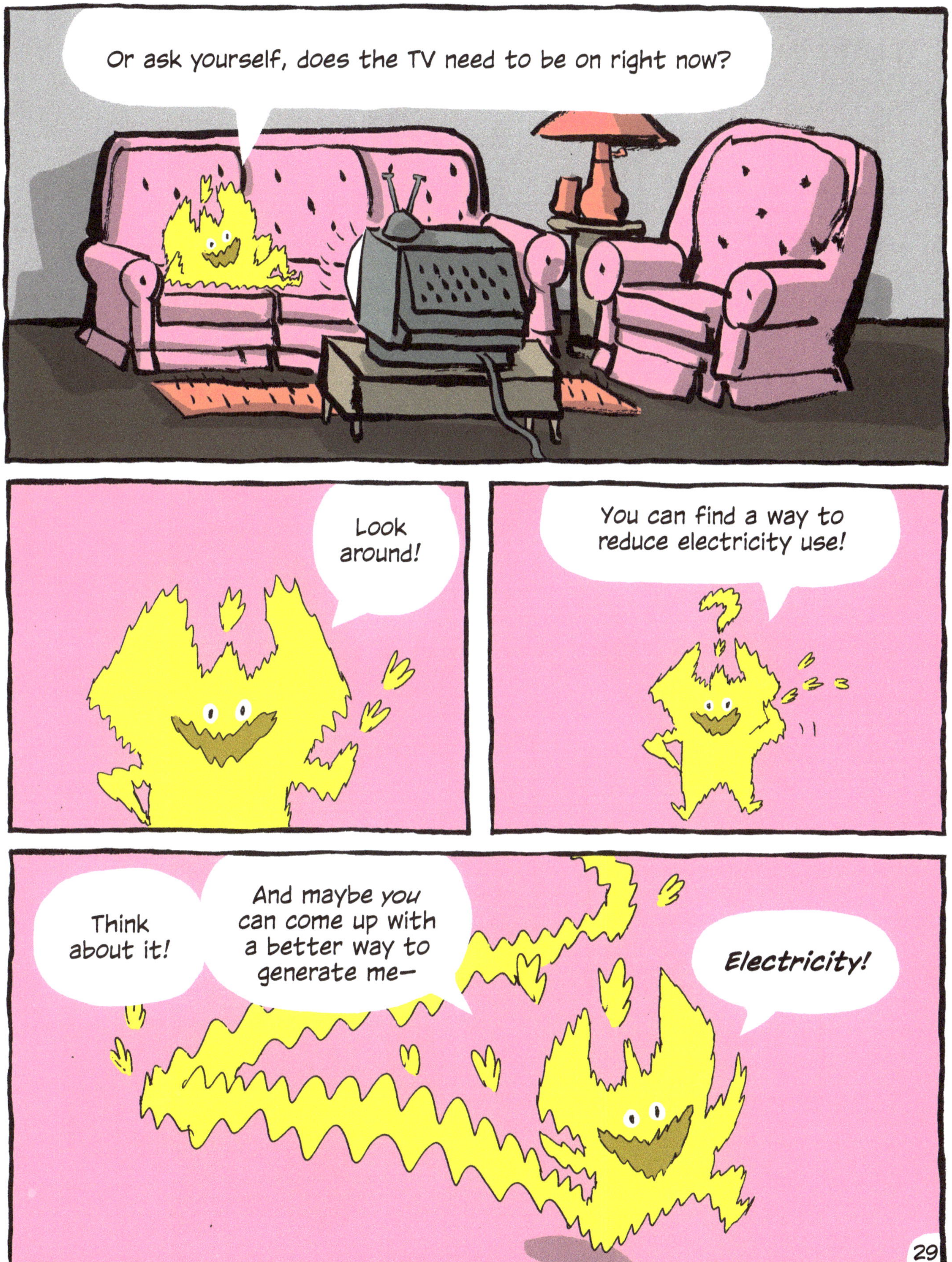

Or ask yourself, does the TV need to be on right now?

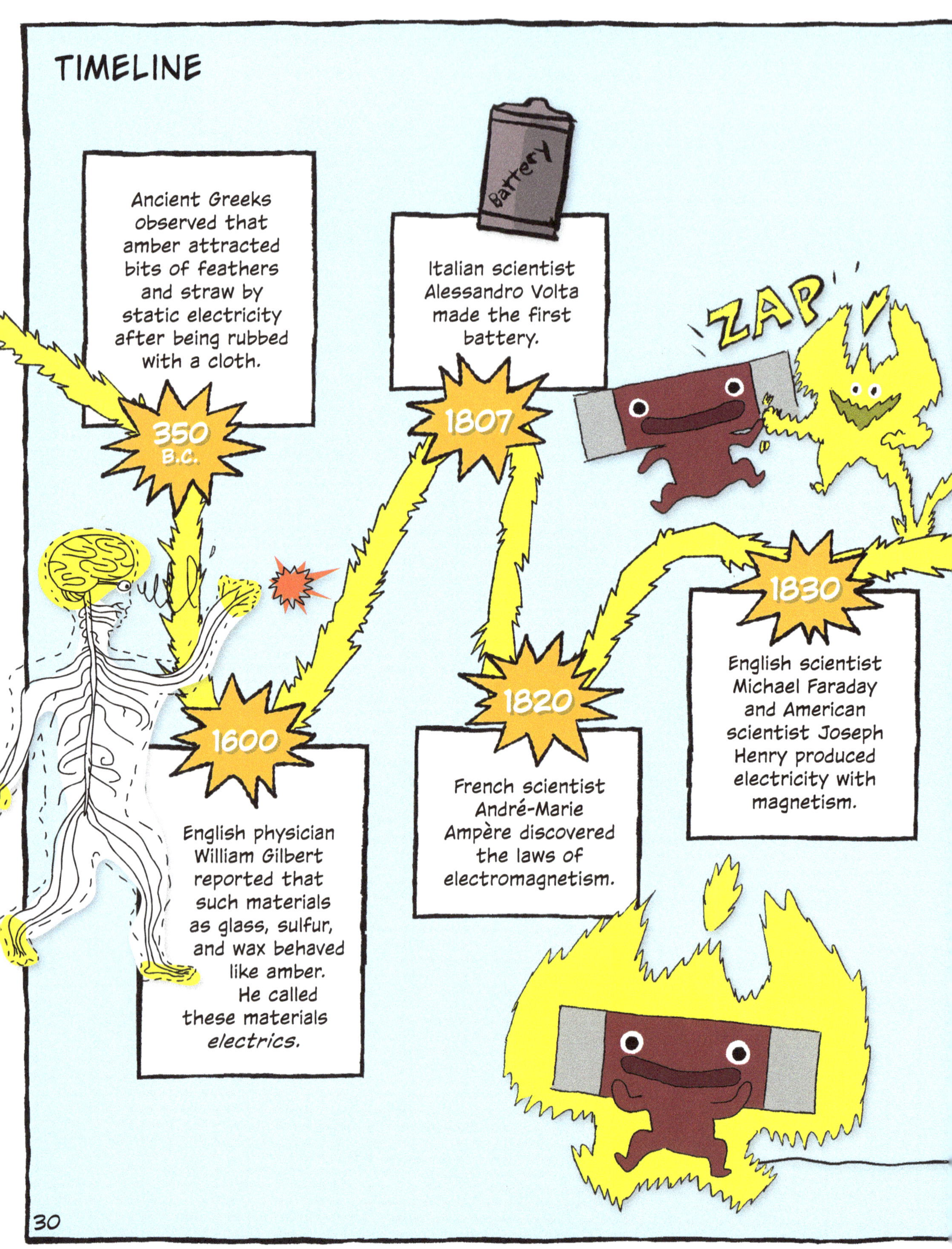
TIMELINE
350 B.C.
Ancient Greeks observed that amber attracted bits of feathers and straw by static electricity after being rubbed with a cloth.
1600
English physician William Gilbert reported that such materials as glass, sulfur, and wax behaved like amber. He called these materials *electrics*.
Battery
1807
Italian scientist Alessandro Volta made the first battery.
1820
French scientist André-Marie Ampère discovered the laws of electromagnetism.
ZAP
1830
English scientist Michael Faraday and American scientist Joseph Henry produced electricity with magnetism.

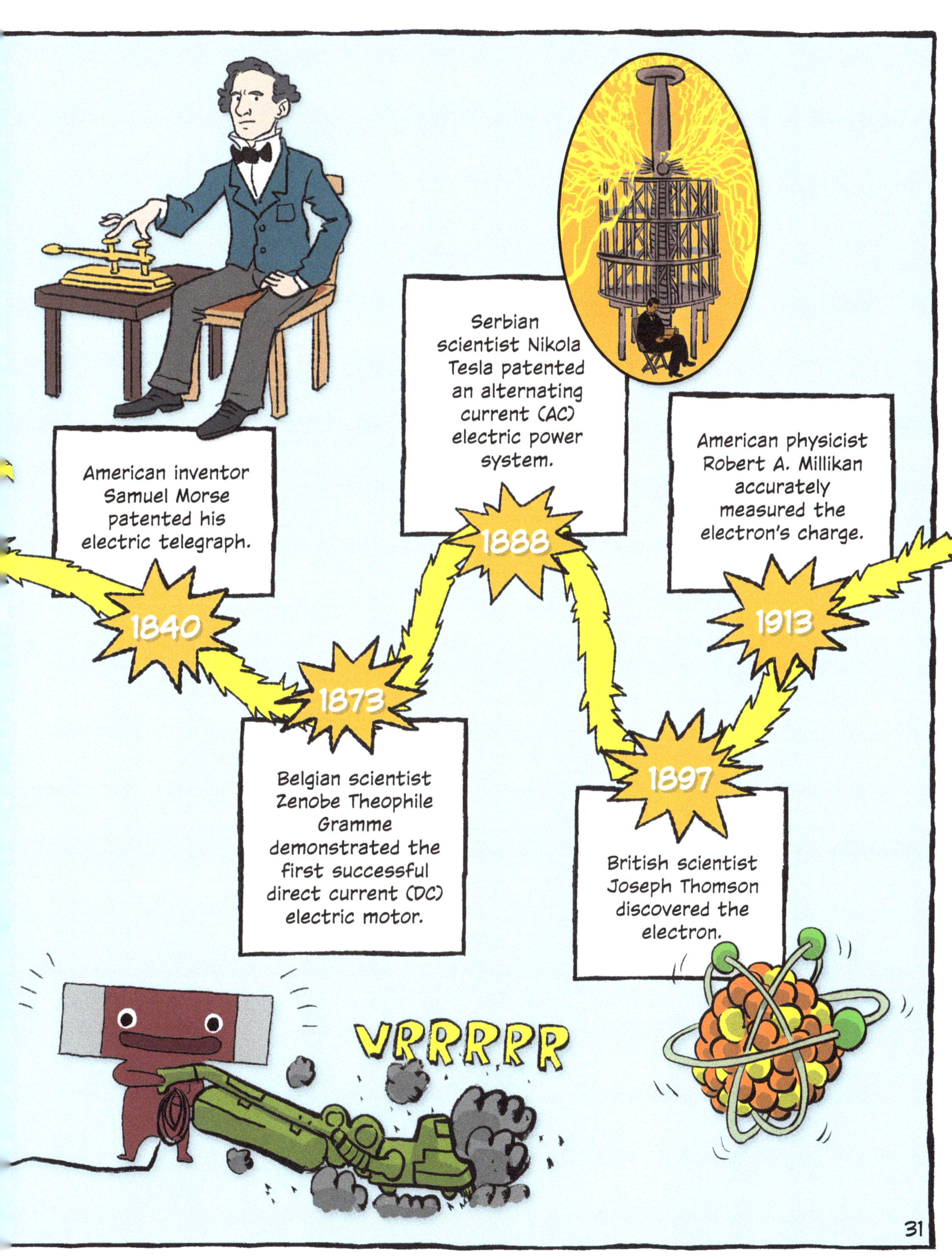
American inventor Samuel Morse patented his electric telegraph.
1840
1873
Belgian scientist Zenobe Theophile Gramme demonstrated the first successful direct current (DC) electric motor.
Serbian scientist Nikola Tesla patented an alternating current (AC) electric power system.
1888
1897
British scientist Joseph Thomson discovered the electron.
American physicist Robert A. Millikan accurately measured the electron's charge.
1913
VRRRRR

ACTIVITY:
HAIR-RAISING ELECTRICITY!

Try this hair-raising experiment to see the effects of static electricity!

What You'll Need

- A balloon
- A short piece of string
- A small cloth, preferably wool
- Hair!

Blow up a balloon and tie it closed with a piece of string. Hold the string up, so the balloon hangs down freely.

When you rub the balloon gently with a wool cloth, the balloon picks up electrons from the cloth. The balloon then has more electrons compared with the cloth.

When you place the cloth next to the balloon and let go of the string, the electrons begin to move back to the cloth. They pull so hard that the balloon sticks to the cloth!

That's static electricity at work!

Now try rubbing the balloon against the hair on your head! Once again, electrons are on the move. This time they are moving from your hair to the balloon.

Gently pull the balloon straight up and away from your hair. You'll see your own hair stand up on end!

CAN YOU BELIEVE IT?!

The **first successful electric car** was built in 1891 by American inventor William Morrison.

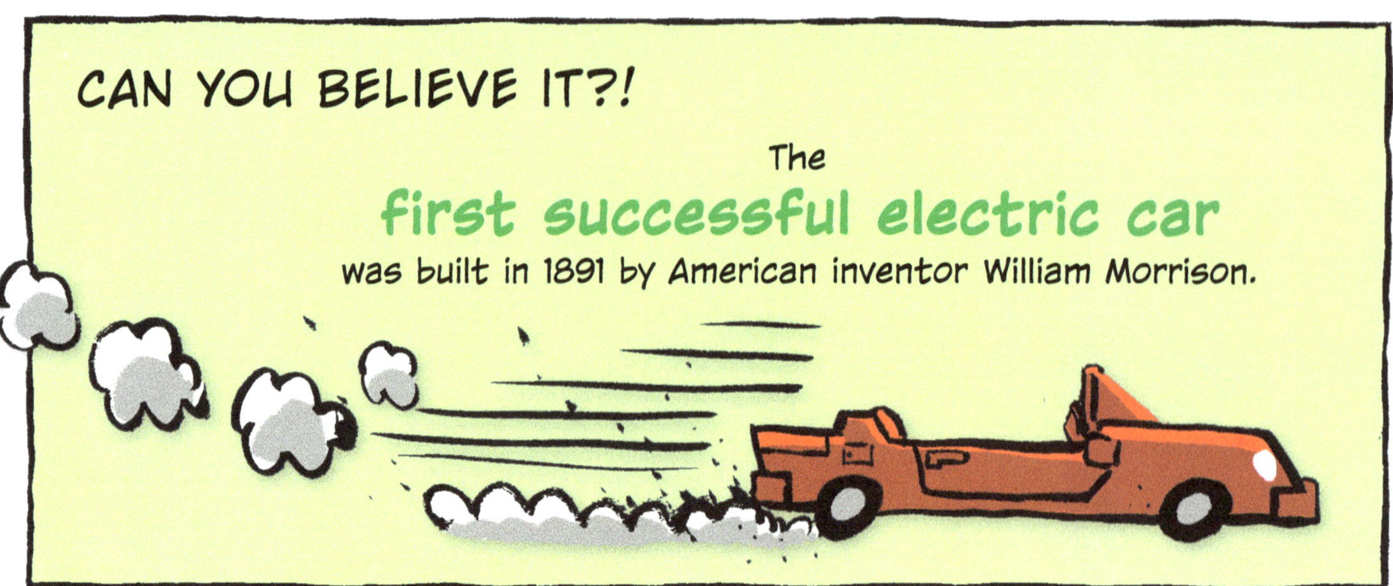

Lightning rods attract lightning away from buildings and down into the ground.

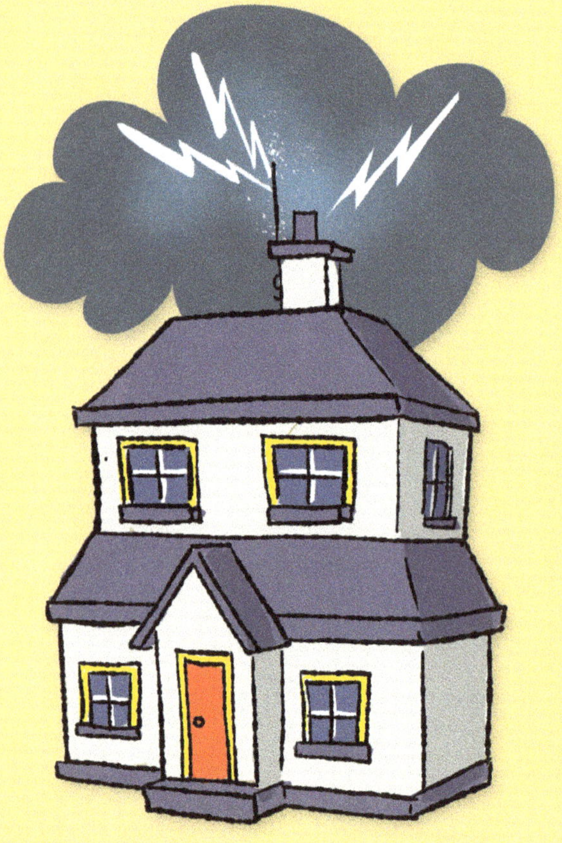

An **electric eel** can produce an electric shock of up to 850 volts!

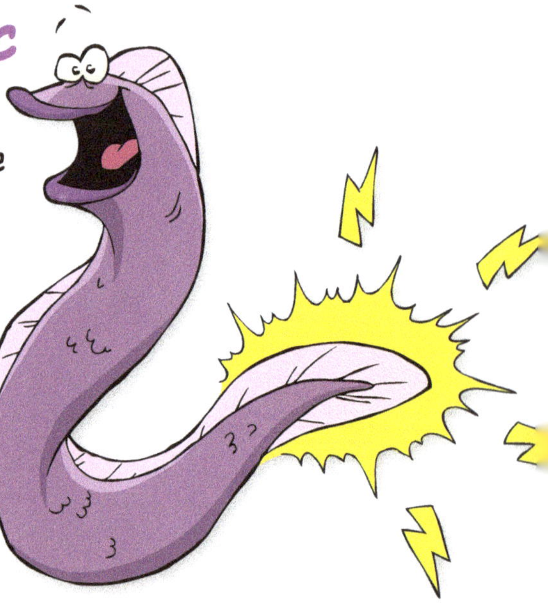

Electricity travels at the **speed of light,** about 186,000 miles per second (300,000 kilometers) per second!

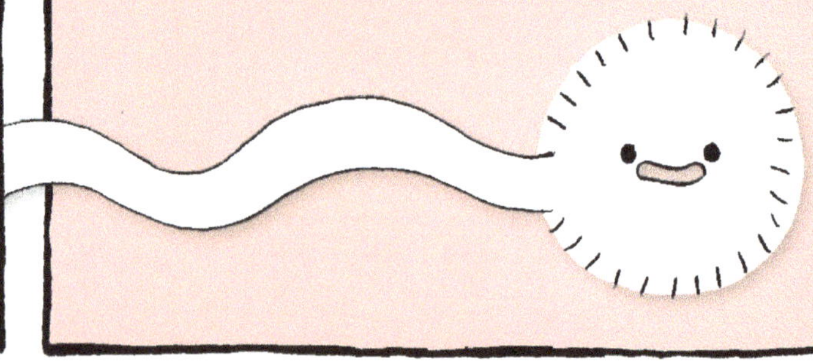

Lightning occurs within the clouds of the planet **Jupiter.**

The first electric **lighthouse** was built in 1858 in England.

A lightning bolt can reach temperatures of about 55,000 °F (30,000 °C)! That's hotter than the **surface of the sun!**

A typical lightning bolt may reach **100 million volts!**

Your brain sends millions of **electrical signals** along the nerves in your nervous system every second!

WHO'S WHO:
THOMAS EDISON vs. NIKOLA TESLA
Hey there! You look familiar!
I'm Thomas Edison. I perfected the incandescent light bulb and created the first electric company.
I am Nikola Tesla, gentleman scientist. I created a power system based on the principle of alternating current.
...Is that Tesla over there?!? Pay him no mind! He's just a disgruntled former employee.
In an AC system, the current changes direction dozens of times per second.
Whoa!

But nothing can *use* AC, you pompous windbag! Only direct current, where the charge flows in one direction, is of any use.
Whee!
Ah, Edison, you old fool! AC is far more practical. It is easier to produce, can be boosted to higher voltages, and can cross long distances.
Fellas, please! You're *both* right!
But it's dangerous! Do you even care what a jolt of AC can do to–

AC is better for moving electricity over long distances.
But many things people use every day need DC.
Phenomenal!
Converters like these change alternating current into direct current.
Ingenious!
Fact File
Name: Thomas Edison
Born: 1847 in Milan, Ohio, USA
Occupation: Inventor and businessman
Claim to fame: Perfected the incandescent light bulb and many other electrical inventions.
Fact File
Name: Nikola Tesla
Born: 1856 in Smiljan, Austria-Hungary (now in Croatia)
Occupation: Inventor and scientist
Claim to fame: Developed electrical systems that produced and used alternating current.

WORDS TO KNOW

atom one of the basic units of matter.

circuit a path for electric current. A circuit is usually made of metal wire.

conductor something that allows heat, electricity, light, sound, or another form of energy to pass through it.

electric charge a build-up of electricity.

electric current a steady flow of electrons through a material, most commonly a metal.

electric generator a machine that produces electric power from mechanical energy (motion).

electric motor a machine that produces mechanical energy (motion) from electric power.

electron a kind of particle that circles around the nucleus (center) of an atom. Electrons have a negative electric charge.

fossil fuel a fuel formed from the long-dead remains of living things. Fossil fuels include coal, natural gas, and petroleum (oil).

insulator something that prevents the passage of electricity, heat, or sound.

matter what all things are made of.

metal any of a large group of elements that includes copper, gold, iron, lead, silver, tin, and other elements that share similar qualities.

motion a change in position.

nuclear fuel a material that releases energy created by the splitting of its atoms.

solar of the sun.

static electricity the build-up of electrons on the surface of an object.

switch a device that opens or closes a gap in a circuit.

turbine an engine or motor in which a wheel is made to revolve by the force of water, steam, hot gases, or air. Turbines are often used to turn generators that produce electric power.

INDEX

www.ingramcontent.com/pod-product-compliance
Lightning Source LLC
LaVergne TN
LVHW060633110826
845147LV00014B/902
* 9 7 8 0 7 1 6 6 5 0 5 4 6 *